THE GOLDEN YEARS

1955

text: David Sandison

design: Paul Kurzeja

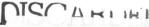

§

SIENA

1955

I f any one word sums up the world in 1955, it must be 'turmoil'. No matter where you turn, change was being fought for as bitterly as it was being resisted by those who wanted to maintain the *status quo*.

With his health already poor, it's easy to understand why Sir Winston Churchill decided to quit the world stage in 1955 and hand the reins of power to a younger, fitter man. Anthony Eden was also given a whole heap of international headaches as various members of the British Commonwealth witnessed increasingly-bloody resistance to UK rule. Successive French governments tried unsuccessfully to meet the demands of Algerian and Moroccan nationalists prepared to burn, bomb and kill their way to independence. The black majority in South Africa learned that the white apartheid regime was also ready to do its share of burning and killing to protect its way of life.

Racial issues loomed large elsewhere. In the United States, black citizens in Alabama were forced to take direct passive action to claim the rights to which the US Supreme Court had ruled they were entitled in law. In Britain, white workers fought less passively against working alongside the many West Indians arriving in what they'd been

5

told was a land of unlimited opportunity.

World tennis fans mourned the early retirement of the wondrous Maureen 'Little Mo' Connolly, the game's first modern superstar. Jazz lost the rare and precious talent of Charlie Parker, and a generation of teenagers had James Dean taken from them, just as they accepted him as an idol.

But there was good news. After initial glitches, Jonas Salk's polio vaccine began to put an end to the deadly virus. And the arrival of rock 'n' roll, in the shape of Bill Haley's Rock Around The Clock, would give us all a new soundtrack to help blow away any blues the news may cause.

Snooker Ace Davis Scores TV First

Compared to the hundreds of hours devoted to the sport by television worldwide today, coverage of snooker in 1955 Britain was restricted mainly to the occasional inclusion of a few edited highlights of major championships.

Due partly to snooker's slightly disreputable reputation, the fierce competition for airtime on the country's sole TV channel, and partly by the obvious handicap of monochrome pictures, it's not surprising the BBC paid scant attention.

Fury As Kenyan Government Offers Mau Mau Amnesty

EUROPEAN KENYANS REACTED BITTERLY and furiously today to an offer of amnesty made to Mau Mau terrorists by the Governor, Sir Evelyn Baring. He has told members of the pro-independence organization - most of them Kikuyu tribesmen - that they would not be hanged if they surrendered at once, although they could be held in detention.

His announcement brought a sharp response from the previously-moderate Legislative Council member, Humphrey Slade: 'This means that men who have killed inoffensive civilians by panga slashing, men who have disembowelled babies before their mothers' eyes, men who have eaten the brains of their human victims, will not even be prosecuted.'

Sworn to secrecy on pain of death, Mau Mau terrorists have waged a bloody war against white farmers and settlers for the past three and a half years, surviving the 1952 arrest and imprisonment of their leader Jomo 'Burning Spear' Kenyatta and the capture, in 1954, of generals known as China, Katanga and Tanganyika, and the mass arrest of 40,000 suspected guerillas and sympathizers when a previous amnesty offer failed.

Although the main targets of their campaign are whites, the Mau Mau have also subjugated many black Africans with selective attacks and murders to ensure their silence and cooperation.

US Banks Merge

American and world banking gained a new giant player today when two major US banks announced they are to merge their already-vast interests and infrastructures.

The two are Chase National Bank and The Bank of Manhattan. When consolidation is complete, the new outfit will be known as The Chase Manhattan Bank.

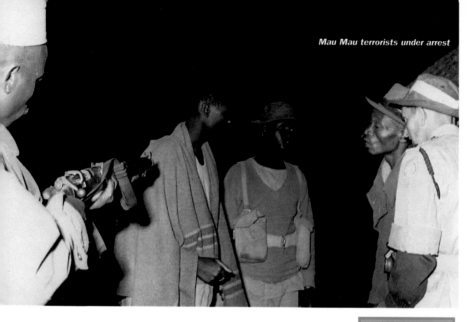

Mau Mau terrorists under arrest

Mitterand Proposes French-Algerian Merger

JANUARY 5

As Algerian nationalists continued their armed campaign to win independence from France, Interior Minister Francois Mitterand emerged today as a hard-liner determined not to lose control over his country's north African colony.

Speaking in Paris, Mitterand went a step further than most when he proposed to end Algeria's colonial status by integrating it completely with France.

Besides attracting the scorn of constitutional experts who cannot see how two nations separated by vastly differing cultures and more than 600 km (400 miles) of the Mediterranean could possibly share a common Paris-based government which would be almost 1400k from Algiers, Mitterand's scheme will be flatly rejected by Ahmed Ben Bella, the Algerian terrorist leader.

Based in the Egyptian capital, Cairo, Ben Bella made his intentions - and his methods of achieving them - clear in November last year when he launched his first series of attacks on French military and police targets in the Aures district, leaving seven dead and a number of farmsteads destroyed.

5

NEWS IN BRIEF

1: The Vickers Valiant, Britain's first A-bomb carrying aircraft, entered service with the RAF

10: Marian Anderson became the first black singer to perform at New York's Metropolitan Opera House; In South Africa, African National Congress leaders announced protests against planned evictions of blacks from Johannesburg

23: In crash of York-Bristol express train at Sutton Coldfield, England, 17 people killed and 43 injured

25: In London, British government unveiled a £1,240 million ($3,730m) rail electrification plan

31: In New York, RCA technology researchers demonstrated a music 'synthesiser'.

WHO Confirm Nuclear Waste Risk

The world's growing pile of nuclear waste could prove a serious health risk to present and future generations, the World Health Organization confirmed today in Switzerland.

A new WHO report reinforces the need for the debris of atomic power development and weapons research to be collected and stored in conditions which will keep it isolated from the environment for many hundreds of years.

According to the report, atomic waste will continue to pose a threat for at least that long. The environmental damage - and potentially fatal consequences to human and animal life - make the creation of secure, almost-eternal storage an international priority.

Mixed Signals As West Indians Arrive In Britain

ALTHOUGH THE OFFICIAL government line says that Britain welcomes the increased numbers of West Indian immigrants arriving to find work, the truth is that many are meeting prejudice at every turn and learning that, even when they do get a job, the relatively high cost of living makes it impossible for them to save the money they'd planned to send home to families they'd left behind.

Today, 380 Jamaican immigrants - all of whom had paid more than £80 ($240) for the 20-day trans-Atlantic voyage - were greeted ashore at the Devon port of Plymouth by a ship's band. They follow 400 others who arrived in London two weeks ago.

Many of the immigrants, some of whom are skilled but all of whom are prepared to take whatever work they are offered, are joining families and friends already in Britain. However, some are complaining that the picture they were painted of life in Britain was false.

Today's arrivals travelled on the liner *Fairsea* (pictured) , which has been adapted for immigration traffic with 60-berth dormitories. Described by her skipper, Captain George Gladioli, as 'among the cleanest, most respectable and intelligent passengers I have ever carried', they were taken by train to London to be met by several hundred other Jamaicans. Widespread public concern about the number of West Indians arriving with little or no money, an increase in a 'no blacks' policy by landlords and the refusal of some people to work with black colleagues, have all led to pressure on the government to introduce controls.

Boffins Admit Piltdown Hoax

British archaeologists today admitted what they'd actually known for almost two years: the 'Piltdown Man' skull, which generations of schoolkids had been told was the missing link between Man and his ape ancestors, was a complete fake. The skull was 'discovered' in 1912 during a dig in the village of Piltdown, near the Sussex town of Lewes and appeared to have the distinctive characteristics of both ape and human. Tests by scientists using procedures not available when the skull was first presented to London's Natural History Museum and put on prominent display, had proved that Piltdown Man was a union of parts of different creatures from widely-separated historical periods. The archaeology establishment had been too embarrassed to confess the hoax until now.

Russia: Malenkov Quits, Bulganin In, Khrushchev Supreme

RUSSIANS LEARNED THEY had a new premier today when the USSR's Defense Minister, Marshal Nikolai Bulganin, replaced the Prime Minister of almost two years, Georgi Malenkov. While Bulganin may be the Soviet Union's leader by title, no-one doubts that the real power in the land is now Nikita Khrushchev, First Secretary of the all-powerful Communist Party.

It was Khrushchev who forced Malenkov's surprise step-down during a meeting of the Supreme Soviet. The outgoing premier's letter of resignation said his 'lack of experience' had held back economic progress and vital agricultural production advances.

Khrushchev and Malenkov emerged as the Soviet Union's two main players in the jostling which followed the death of dictator Josef Stalin in March 1953. Although Malenkov came out of the infighting as Prime Minister and First Secretary, he relinquished the party post to Khrushchev, who so became the only man to have a seat on the party secretariat and the ruling Politburo.

With those formidable twin power bases, Khrushchev began steering Soviet policy and establishing himself on the international stage. Even though some of his reforms have relaxed many of the Stalin regime's more repressive aspects, Khrushchev's ousting of Malenkov proves he can be just as ruthless.

Britain Goes Nuclear

Anti-nuclear lobbyists in Britain had a lean time of it this month as the government put itself firmly down on the side of nuclear-derived power and the development of a bigger set of British bombs.

On February 15 it was announced that the UK intends to build 12 nuclear power stations in the next decade, spending around £300 million ($900m) in the process. February 17 saw the publication of a defense paper which confirmed that Britain is now manufacturing hydrogen bombs as part of an Anglo-US deal which gives UK scientists access to more advanced American know-how.

Tornadoes Mangle Mississippi

The state of Mississippi was hit by a series of tornadoes today as storms raged through the American south, leaving a trail of destruction it is reckoned will cost tens of millions to repair.

Twenty-nine people were reported killed by state authorities, who have called on President Eisenhower to authorize federal funds to aid the disaster zone.

Little Mo Calls It A Day

Teenage tennis ace Maureen 'Little Mo' Connolly (pictured) , who burst on the international championship circuit in 1952 as the 17 year old winner of the Wimbledon tournament, shocked the sports world today when she announced her retirement.

California-born Connolly, who was injured in a car crash recently, intends to marry. Although apparently completely recovered from her injuries, it seems she is not prepared to combine the two careers of sports star and wife.

Junior US champion before she made her victorious Wimbledon debut and became the youngest women's title-holder since 15 year old Lottie Dod beat all-comers in 1887, Little Mo won the All-England championships three years in succession, along with many other international contests.

ARRIVALS
Born this month:
9: Jimmy Pursey, UK rock musician (Sham 69)
10: Greg Norman, Australian golf champion
24: Alain Prost, French world motor-racing champion
27: Gary Christian, UK rock musician (The Christians)

DEPARTURES
Died this month:
23: Paul-Louis-Charles Claudel, French poet, playwright, diplomat

FEBRUARY 10

South Africa Evicts 60,000 Township Blacks

THE SOUTH AFRICAN government today carried out its threatened destruction of the black Johannesburg township of Sophiatown and the enforced eviction of its 60,000 inhabitants, when 3,000 armed police moved in ahead of bulldozers.

The destruction of Sophiatown, situated in west Johannesburg, follows the white Nationalist Government's recent decision to designate it a whites-only residential area and so expand a neighboring white suburb.

As the population began the move to the new township of Meadowlands 11 miles away, Sten gun-bearing police set about razing their homes. Many of these were freeholdings, but everyone will be a tenant in Meadowlands and there will be no compensation for their losses.

Barred from staging strikes or holding public meetings, the African National Congress opposition intends to protest with a series of 'Days of Prayer' to keep its mostly black followers from work.

Algerian Crisis Ousts French PM

French Prime Minister Pierre Mendes-France was turfed out of office today, victim of the growing tensions in Algeria.

France also has problems with its north African colonies of Morocco and Tunisia, and Mendes-France's efforts to steer a middle course of conciliation in the face of local demands for independence, proved too strong for liberals and too weak for conservatives.

Attempting to win a vote of confidence for his chosen course, Mendes-France was defeated in the National Assembly. France's new premier is Edgar Faure, who has pledged to pursue a get-tough policy with dissidents.

UK Follows US Roads Lead

With its house-building programme on track - a record 347,605 new homes were built in 1954 - the British government today followed up its recently announced rail electrification plans with a £212 million ($636m) roads scheme.

A four-year plan, it echoes the United States' multi-billion post-war road modernization programme, the biggest since President Roosevelt's 'New Deal' in the thirties and known to be especially close to President Eisenhower's heart.

New routes are planned between London and Yorkshire, and from Birmingham to Preston, Lancashire. While roads are scheduled to by-pass notorious gridlock towns like Doncaster, Maidenhead and Grantham, critics have slammed the omission of a bridge over the River Severn between England and South Wales, and the lack of a motorway to the Channel ports of Dover and Folkestone.

Israel Attacks Gaza Strip

In a lightning raid believed to be a reprisal for last month's hanging by Egypt of two alleged Jewish spies, Israeli forces claimed to have killed 36 soldiers and six civilians in the Egyptian-held Gaza Strip territory today. The attack, which is the first major violation of the 1949 armistice to end open warfare in Palestine, dealt a severe blow to Egyptian aspirations to leadership of the Arab world and their hopes for a united front against Anglo-US defense policies in the Middle East. Egyptian leader Colonel Gamal Abdel Nasser lodged an immediate protest at Israel's attack and called for his northern neighbours to be censured by the United Nations.

Jazz Genius Parker Dies

THE JAZZ WORLD LOST one of its most innovative and influential performers today when Charlie Parker (pictured), the alto sax player at the very heart of the Bebop revolution which transformed American and world jazz in the 1940s, died in the New York apartment of his long-time fan and socialite friend, the Baroness Nina de Koenigswater. He was 34 years old.

Born in Kansas City, Parker - nicknamed 'Bird' or 'Yardbird' - moved to New York in the early forties, where he found kindred adventurous spirits in musicians like trumpeters Dizzy Gillespie and Miles Davis, pianist Thelonius Monk, guitarist Charlie Christian and drummer Kenny Clarke. Jamming and recording together, they and others pushed the boundaries back with a free-wheeling music which attracted vilification from the old guard but the excited admiration of a younger generation of fans and musicians.

A long-time heroin user and alcoholic, Parker was bound to die tragically young. His influence lives on via his recordings and the inspiration he continues to give to jazz players not even born when he broke the rules to set new standards in musical development and improvisation.

Busmen Impose Colour Bar

The steadily-increasing flow of West Indian immigrants to Britain *(see January)* has finally led to an official colour bar by white British workers unwilling to have black colleagues and alarmed at what they view as an invasion of unwelcome additions to the workforce.

Bus crews in the Midlands town of West Bromwich today announced their introduction of an official ban on immigrant co-workers. An unofficial bar had been in force for some time, and a number of limited-action strikes had already been called before this first public example of the prejudice which immigrants have been claiming confronts them at every turn.

London Bids To End Smog

Smog, the often-deadly mix of smoke and fog in cities which allow the use of 'dirty' coal in domestic fires and unfiltered industrial chimneys, hit London heavily in the winter of 1953. The issue of surgical smog masks to those at greatest risk - people with respiratory or heart problems - did little to help the dozens who died during that November.

Today saw the welcome, if a little late, announcement Londoners had been praying and lobbying to hear. From the beginning of October, Britain's capital will become a 'smokeless zone' when the compulsory use of smoke-free anthracite is introduced.

Environmentalists are now pushing for stricter controls on industrial emissions they say make an equally great contribution to the smog problem.

ARRIVALS

Born this month:
2: Jay Osmond, US pop singer, musician (The Osmonds)
8: David Wilkie, British swimmer, Olympic Gold medallist (Montreal 1976)
10: Bunny DeBarge, US pop musician (DeBarge)
13: Bruno Conti, Italian football star
14: Boon Gould, UK rock musician (Level 42)

DEPARTURES

Died this month:
11: Sir Alexander Fleming, British Nobel Prize-winning bacteriologist *(see main story)*
12: Charlie Parker, US modern jazz pioneer *(see main story)*

No News Is Bad News

It's a fact that Britain publishes, and Britons read, more national newspapers per capita than any other country. So the complete absence of papers from corner stores and newsstands today was bad news for Britain's print junkies.

They'd have to put up with withdrawal symptoms for close on a month as a strike of 700 electricians and maintenance engineers dragged on, only ending on April 21 with a compromise settlement of their pay rise demands.

The men's representatives from the Amalgamated Engineering Union and the Electrical Trades Union had rejected arbitration on their call for a pay hike of £2 18s 6d (almost $9) a week.

2: Floods in Australia claimed 400 lives, left 44,000 homeless and drowned 300,000 sheep in New South Wales

4: In London, The Burnham Committee recommended equal pay for women teachers

13: South African Airways took delivery of the first production model of the British-made *Bristol Britannia* turbo-prop

16: British Labour Party MPs voted to withdraw the party whip from long-time rebel Aneurin Bevan

24: In New York, rave reviews greeted the premiere of Tennessee Williams' new play *Cat On A Hot Tin Roof*

26: Britain's Grand National steeplechase won by Quare Times

MARCH 20

High School Drama Launches Rock

IN NEW YORK, the premiere of a tough drama of a high school teacher's battle with surly students did more than give Glenn Ford one of his grittiest roles and raise the profile of a young actor called Sidney Poitier. *The Blackboard Jungle* also exposed moviegoers to a song called *Rock Around The Clock* to help begin the single biggest explosion of change in modern popular culture.

Although the song had been recorded and released in 1954 by former country and western singer Bill Haley and his band, The Comets (pictured), it had not been as successful as Haley's previous attempts to marry black rhythm and blues with a more commercial white sound, the biggest of which was his Top 10 hit *Shake, Rattle And Roll.*

A number of other white artists, including a young Elvis Presley, had also scored with their hybrids. But the use of *Rock Around The Clock* over the end credits of *The Blackboard Jungle* brought the new music to a vast worldwide audience. They made it a multi-million seller and demanded more of this exciting stuff called rock 'n' roll.

Churchill Denies Yalta Climbdown

MARCH 16

British Prime Minister Sir Winston Churchill today reacted angrily to American politicians' claims that he hadn't fought Soviet leader Josef Stalin hard enough to secure Poland's independence during the 1945 Yalta Conference at which the US, Soviet and British war leaders agreed the future shape of the post-WWII world.

Sir Winston denied that he had not done everything he could to restore democracy to Poland. His view, expressed more candidly now than in the past, is that President Roosevelt - in bad health and only two months away from death - had been the one who submitted to Stalin's demands because he wanted Russian help to ensure the end of the war with Japan.

Penicillin Pioneer Fleming Dead

Sir Alexander Fleming, who died today at the age of 74, was the first to admit that the discovery he made in 1928 - a bacteria-killing mould which would eventually provide medical science with the invaluable life-saving penicillin - owed as much to chance as it did to his research work at London's St. Mary's Hospital.

Investigating the growth of germs, the professor left a plate of bacteria out in his laboratory for a few days. Inspecting it, he discovered that rings had formed around the mould to apparently kill the bacteria.

Identifying the mould as Penicillium Notatum, Fleming and others began work on creating a vaccine which would attack, kill or halt the progress of deadly bacteria in animals and humans.

Fleming was awarded the Nobel Prize in 1945 for his work, fitting recognition for a discovery which had saved countless millions of lives.

OSCAR AWARDS SWEEP FOR SMALL BUDGET LITTLE GUYS

Let's face it, while the annual Academy Awards ceremony does have a degree of tension as TV cameras close in on Oscar nominees trying to put on a brave face in what must be unbearable moments of pure terror, the usual questions are: which highly-paid megastar will beat the other four household name superstars nominated, or which zillion-dollar budget epic will steal it from the other squillion-buck productions in contention?

Now and again, however, the Academy of Motion Pictures Arts and Sciences does turn Warren Beatty's observation ('The Golden Globes are fun. The Oscars are business') on its well-turned head and give its highest honours to producers, directors, actors and writers who really have made the year's best movies, and have done so with costs which wouldn't keep the average studio boss in silk suits.

In 1954 the Academy did it with *On The Waterfront* (which cost less than $1million), and this year did it again with the beautiful, tender and timeless *Marty,* whose producers spent more promoting its Oscar nominations than they did creating this little masterpiece.

Starring Ernest Borgnine and Betsy Blair, directed by Delbert Mann and written by Paddy Chayefsky, *Marty* won Oscars for Borgnine, Mann and Chayefsky, as well as the Best Picture trophy and a well-deserved

Supporting Actress nomination for Blair, who lost out to Jo Van Fleet, who won it for her work on *East Of Eden.*

That, of course, signalled the screen arrival of James Dean, who duly won a Best Actor nomination for his debut while Elia Kazan picked up a Best Director listing to follow up his 1954 *Oscar for Waterfront.*

Although Dean was not nominated for his second big hit of the year, *Rebel Without A Cause,* his co-stars Sal Mineo and Natalie Wood both appeared in the short-lists as supporting actor and actress. Mineo lost out to an on-form Jack Lemmon, who helped make the navy drama *Mister Roberts* a Best Picture nominee.

Competition for Best Actress Oscar was tough. Nominations included Susan Hayward in the powerful drama *I'll Cry Tomorrow,* Katharine Hepburn *(Summertime)* and Jennifer Jones *(Love Is A Many-Splendored Thing)*, but the prize was picked up by tempestuous Italian actress Anna Magnani, whose forceful performance in the Best Picture-nominated *The Rose Tattoo* would make her Oscar one of the best-deserved in years.

Borgnine's award killed any hopes Frank Sinatra had of topping his 1953 Supporting Actor Oscar for *From Here To Eternity,* with a Best Actor prize for his excellent junkie jazzman in *The Man With The Golden Arm,* while the one-armed WWII veteran portrayed by Spencer Tracy in *Bad Day At Black Rock* would have probably

won him the title any other year.

The box-office success of *Love Is A Many-Splendored Thing* was recognized by the Oscars awarded to Alfred Newman (Best Drama Score), Sammy Fain and Paul Francis Webster (Original Song) and Charles LeMaire (Color Costume Design).

As it had already appeared successfully on-stage, Rodgers and Hammerstein's *Oklahoma!* was barred from the Original Song category it probably would have walked with any one of six numbers, so the awards given to Robert Russell Bennet, Jay Blackton and Adolph Deutsch (for Musical Picture Score) and Fred Hynes of the Todd-AO Sound Department (Best Sound) were reasonable reward.

But the real and biggest rewards went to the just, just for a welcome change.

James Dean, Natalie Wood and Sal Mineo in Rebel Without a Cause.

APRIL 5

Churchill Resigns, Eden New Prime Minister

SIR WINSTON CHURCHILL, Britain's leader during WWII, amateur painter, Nobel Prize-winning historian and one of the most influential world statesmen of the 20th century, today announced his resignation as British Prime Minister at the age of 80. His successor as PM and leader of the Conservative Party is to be Sir Anthony Eden, the former Foreign Secretary.

Hit by a stroke in June 1953, news which British newspaper owners conspired to keep secret from their readers, and increasingly frail, Churchill decided to quit now to ensure the hand-over of power was achieved smoothly.

Sir Winston will stay on in Parliament, where his debating skills will be used from the back benches. They are still formidable - his March 1 speech in defence of Britain's H-bomb was a memorable *tour de force* in which he said possession of the bomb would ensure that 'safety will be the sturdy child of terror'.

Sir Anthony's first cabinet would include Harold Macmillan as Foreign Secretary and R.A. Butler as Chancellor of the Exchequer.

The new PM wasted no time in confronting the opposition and attempting to secure himself a new mandate. Eden followed an April 19 budget - which cut basic income tax by sixpence (18 cents) and increased tax allowances - with an April 22 announcement of a General Election, to be held on May 26, and stressed his intention of ensuring a property and share-owning democracy.

Labour would use their election manifesto to attack the rising cost of living and renew calls for international talks on the H-bomb aimed at multi-lateral disarmament.

Mau Mau Kill Two Schoolboys

White Kenyan revulsion at the murderous activities of the independence-seeking Mau Mau organization was heightened today with the discovery of the bodies of two English schoolboys. Like so many of the Mau Mau's victims of the past three years, the boys had been hacked to death with pangas, the traditional machete-knife favoured by the Kikuyu tribe. The boys, holidaying in Kenya with relatives, are a tragic reminder that the Mau Mau do not discriminate the age at which Europeans become the enemy. Although the Mau Mau's imprisoned leader Jomo Kenyatta has denied his movement is anti-white, local authorities are quick to point out that the boys' only crime appears to have been their skin colour.

Polio Vaccine Gets Green Light

The new anti-polio vaccine first developed by American scientist Dr Jonas Salk in 1953 and the subject of nationwide trials since February last year, was given the all-clear today by doctors evaluating the tests from the Department of Epidemiology at the University of Michigan's School of Health.

After an initial glitch in production of the vaccine at the University of Toronto, the year-long trial began. Consisting of 'blind' tests using Salk's vaccine and placebo injections, a coding system ensured that final results would not be known until now.

Convinced by the figures, the Michigan board have given Salk's vaccine the green light and said that its widespread use can begin soon.

Super-Scientist Einstein Dies

Albert Einstein, the German-born physicist whose 1905 thesis, *The Theory of Special Relativity*, helped make him the world's best-known (if least understood) scientist, died today in Princeton, New Jersey. He was 76 years old. *(For a full appreciation, see Came & Went pages)*

ARRIVALS

Born this month:
17: Pete Shelley (Peter McNeice), UK rock musician (Buzzcocks)
23: Tony Miles, UK chess grandmaster; Mike Smith, UK disc jockey, TV host
25: Dr. John Nunn, UK chess grandmaster; Christopher 'Buster' Mottram, English Davis Cup tennis player

DEPARTURES

Died this month:
7: Theda Bara (Theadasia Goodman), US silent screen vamp
18: Albert Einstein, German-born, US-based physicist *(see Came & Went pages)*

1: In Hamburg, the German national airline Lufthansa, inoperative since 1945, was re-born

3: Mexico mourned the death of over 300 killed when a train crashed into a canyon near Guadalajara

4: Chinese secret police arrested Manchurian Communist Party leader Kao-kang, dismissed and charged with plotting to overthrow Mao Tse-Tung

16: The Council of Europe admitted Austria to membership

18: A new neutral zone established in Jerusalem by Jordan and Israel authorities; Hungarian premier Imre Nagy dismissed and accused of 'deviation' - replaced by Andras Hegedus

APRIL 29

Saigon Ablaze As Civil War Rages

SAIGON'S CHINESE SUBURB of Cholon was in flames tonight and 160 were reported killed as the South Vietnamese capital became the battlefield in a civil war between factions pro or anti the government of Emperor Bao Dai, ruling from luxury exile in a French Riviera villa.

Leading the anti-Bao brigade is the French-backed Binh Xuyen movement. The Bao government is supported by the United States, and it was an attack by government paratroops and tanks against dug-in Binh Xuyen forces which caused today's casualties.

The confrontation was inspired by a Binh Xuyen mortar bomb assault on the palace of Prime Minister Ngo Dinh Diem after he fired Saigon's police chief, one of the quasi-religious sect's leaders. The premier ordered his forces to retaliate.

As ever, the background to the war is complex and has a fair hint of corruption. General Nguyen Van Vy, the dismissed police chief, is reputed to have made his fortune during the Japanese occupation of Vietnam during WWII, when he controlled all the brothels and casinos in Cholon. And while the Binh Xuyen claim to have Buddhism as their inspirational base, the sect actually began life as notoriously brutal river pirates.

Former Model Charged With Ex-Lover's Murder

With British newspapers back on sale, today's headlines were devoted to a story with all the vital ingredients for record sales: a beautiful blonde, a fast-living, handsome racing driver, high society drinking clubs - and murder most foul.

Sent for trial at London's Old Bailey was ex-model platinum blonde Ruth Ellis (pictured), the 28 year old former manageress of a swish Knightsbridge drinking club. She is accused of shooting racing driver David Blakely, her one-time lover, outside a pub on London's Hampstead Heath on Easter Sunday. Besides giving the country a chance to revel in gory details when the case comes to court in June, the trial will also revive the capital punishment debate.

If Ellis is found guilty of firing the two bullets which hit Blakely in the back, she could be sentenced to death. In February, capital punishment was retained as the ultimate sanction when an anti-hanging bill was defeated in Parliament.

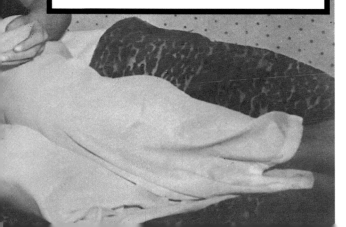

3 Million Scots Hear Graham's Message

Encouraged by the phenomenal success of his first visit to Britain last year when his London Crusade reached a triumphant climax with 180,000 packing Wembley Stadium in May, American evangelist Dr Billy Graham has returned - targetting Scotland this time.

His six-week crusade ended in Glasgow today with the charismatic Christian having attracted more than 3 million to his meetings nationwide.

APRIL

MAY

Tito And Khrushchev Mend Seven-Year Rift

The seven-year rift between Yugoslavia and the Soviet Union, begun during the Stalin era, appeared to be mended today when Russian party boss Nikita Khrushchev offered an olive branch and apologies for past attitudes to President Tito at the end of a week-long visit to the Yugoslav capital, Belgrade (pictured).

Observers noted that while Tito seems to have accepted the Russian gesture in good grace, his Yugoslavian regime still wants to keep a careful distance from the USSR and the recently-signed Warsaw Pact. The most they will do is sign a treaty which reinstates friendly relations and expands economic ties with the USSR.

Khrushchev clearly enjoyed his trip, displaying some of the uninhibited behaviour which would so mark his later international career. Official dinners were often used by him to get enthusiastically under the influence of the wines on offer.

Hiroshima Victims Arrive In US

Plastic surgeons were on hand in California today to welcome 25 of the worst-injured survivors of the atomic bomb blast which decimated the Japanese city of Hiroshima in August 1945 and, with the A-bomb attack on Nagasaki, forced an end to WWII.

The 25 are to undergo exhaustive tests to determine just how much the surgeons - all of whom have volunteered their time and skills to the awesome task - can do to repair the terrible injuries they suffered 10 years ago and which Japanese doctors are unable to treat.

Warsaw Pact Unites Eastern Bloc Reds

THE WORLD GAINED A WORRYING new military alliance today when all leading Eastern Bloc communist nations gathered in the Polish capital Warsaw to sign a mutual defense pact which mirrors the North Atlantic Treaty Organization of Western allies.

The Soviet Prime Minister, Marshal Nikolai Bulganin, was first to place his signature on the pact document, followed by representatives of Poland, Czechoslovakia, Rumania, Hungary, East Germany, Bulgaria and Albania. All have agreed to refrain from using force to solve international disagreements and have notionally committed to working towards peace and world disarmament.

The Warsaw Pact gives the Soviet Union the advantage of being able to base its troops in any of the signatory countries, using the slightest evidence of 'aggression' as an excuse to mobilize forces. The Pact's HQ will be in Moscow, with officers from member states reporting to the newly-appointed commander, 58 year-old Marshal Koniev, head of USSR ground forces.

The only Eastern European country not to join the Pact is Yugoslavia. Led by the more enlightened and pragmatic President Josip Tito, it was expelled from the Cominform group of communist nations in 1948 by the Soviet dictator Josef Stalin.

MAY 21

Eden Wins Election In Strike-Bound Britain

WITH STRIKING DOCK WORKERS halting the movement of all imported goods and giving him a great example with which to warn British voters of the dangers of returning a socialist Labour Party to power, Sir Anthony Eden led the Conservative Party back into power today. With an increased overall majority of 58, he has the mandate he demanded.

Labour's defeat was a bitter pill for leader Clement Attlee, who had spent the past year uneasily negotiating for compromise between his party's hardline left wing and those who want to revise policies.

Dirty tricks played their part in the last few days of the election campaign when the Conservatives 'uncovered' a plot in Labour ranks to replace Attlee with hard-left firebrand Aneurin Bevan if they won the election. Labour's denials were strenuous but ultimately pointless, but will help Labour's party treasurer Hugh Gaitskell in his fight to reduce the left-wing's influence.

Sir Anthony was especially full of praise for election work carried out by young party volunteers. 'We are the old party rejuvenated', he told them at celebrations in his party's national headquarters.

The election was also a personal victory for Sir Winston Churchill, whose resignation as PM had ultimately led to Eden's decision to go to the nation. He held on to his Woodford constituency in outer London after campaigning vigorously, cheerfully insulting Labour's leaders at every turn to the delight of partisan crowds.

MAY 31

Supreme Court Orders Southern Integration

Confronted by obdurate and mounting resistance to its historic May 1954 decision that racial segregation in schools should end, the US Supreme Court today responded with an order that southern states must comply. However, the Court stopped short of enforcing a deadline.

The Supreme Court's original pronouncement overturned an 1896 ruling that education could be 'separate but equal'. In his judgment, Chief Justice Earl Warren said racially segregated educational facilities were 'inherently unequal'.

Among those who attacked the Warren ruling was Georgia's Agriculture Commissioner Linder, who said at the time: 'We are going to have segregation regardless of what the court rules'.

MAY 8

Salk Vaccine Withdrawn

The polio vaccine developed by Dr Jonas Salk (pictured), and approved for widespread use only last month, was ordered to be withdrawn today when US medical authorities learned that 41 inoculated people had contracted the potential-killer virus.

Investigations would lead to improvements in the process by which live polio virus samples were rendered harmless in final testing procedures. With those in place, Salk's life-saving discovery could be re-introduced and begin its work of eliminating a worldwide menace.

MAY 31

UK Dockers Clamped By Emergency Powers

Ten days into his new term of office, British Prime Minister Sir Anthony Eden hit back at 60,000 striking dock workers today with an Emergency Powers Act which he can use against anyone threatening to deprive the country of the 'essentials of life' - especially food suplies.

The Act required the Queen's signature to become law, so Eden and members of the Privy Council flew to Balmoral Castle, the royal family's traditional summer holiday retreat in Scotland since Queen Victoria's reign.

Home Secretary Major Lloyd George denied that the proclamation was intended to enable the government to break the strike, which would drag on until July. It was introduced, he said, to ensure the direction of food supplies and maintain public order. Eden's problems had increased on May 29 when 65,000 British Railways staff began a strike over pay differentials - a strike which would end on June 14.

JUNE 21

Ruth Ellis Sentenced To Hang

Ruth Ellis, the glamorous blonde at the heart of the murder case which has dominated British tabloids since her arrest in April, was today found guilty of shooting her ex-lover David Blakely and sentenced to hang.

Evidence against Ellis, the former drinking club hostess stricken by jealousy when Blakely confirmed that their affair was over and he was seeing another woman, was so overwhelming the Old Bailey trial lasted only two days and the jury needed only 25 minutes to reach their verdict.

Ellis used a Smith and Wesson revolver to shoot the former racing driver playboy in the back. It had, she said, been given to her three years earlier as security for a bar debt. She displayed no emotion as Mr Justice Havers pronounced sentence and says she will appeal.

Eighty Killed In Le Mans Horror

THE WORLD IMAGE OF MOTOR RACING was battered today when 80 spectators attending the annual Le Mans 24-hour race in France were killed as three cars ploughed into a grandstand. Unbelievably, officials allowed the event to continue as rescuers clawed through the carnage to drag out the dead and more than 100 injured.

Witnesses to the worst disaster ever to hit a marathon event its critics say is both pointless and dangerous, described the crash site as 'a battlefield', with a 60-yard strip along the track soaked in blood. Among the dead, some of whom were decapitated as one vehicle somersaulted through the crowd, were a number of young children.

The tragedy occurred during the mass start of the endurance race when car speeds had already reached 150 mph (240 kph). One of the three vehicles involved in the initial collision was part of the eventually-victorious Mercedes team whose members gave up their titles after learning one of their cars had been involved.

Pressed to explain his actions, the course director told horrified reporters: 'I did not judge, in spite of the horror of the situation, that the race should be interrupted'.

Mau Mau Killers Guilty Of Schoolboy Deaths

The trial of nine Mau Mau activists for the murder in April of the two English schoolboys found hacked to death, ended in the Kenyan capital Nairobi today with all found guilty and sentenced to death.

Their trial was held in an increasingly tense atmosphere caused by the June 10 withdrawal of the amnesty offered to all Mau Mau members by the British government in January.

New search-and-destroy missions against suspected Mau Mau hide-outs have been mounted by Kenyan and British forces determined to crush the murderous secret society.

ARRIVALS

Born this month:

20: Michael Anthony, US rock musician (Van Halen)

21: Michel Platini, French football star

23: Maggie Philbin, UK TV presenter

25: Victor (Vic) Marks, England cricketer

26: Mick Jones, UK punk rock pioneer (The Clash, Big Audio Dynamite)

JUNE 30

Police Seize Arms Cache In Cyprus Raid

Large amounts of guns, ammunition and explosives were captured by Cypriot police tonight as they mounted lightning raids on terrorist hide-outs and the headquarters of EOKA, the terrorist group fighting for independence from Britain and union with Greece. A number of key EOKA personnel were arrested during an operation which saw British troops mounting roadblocks, RAF planes patrolling the coastline and a British frigate moored in a northern bay.

Earlier this month there were bomb attacks on British military posts in Nicosia and Famagusta, and riots in Larnaca when six Cypriots were jailed for possession of explosives with intent to overthrow the government. Leaders of the island's Turkish community have welcomed Britain's invitation to the Greek and Turkish governments to attend a tripartite conference to discuss and attempt to solve the crisis. However, Greek leaders have insisted on a formal British recognition of eventual self-determination before any conference can go ahead.

JUNE 26

SA Police Break Up Congress Protest

Armed with Sten guns and bayoneted rifles, South African police today broke up a mass-protest Congress of the People in a non-white suburb of Johannesburg. More than 3,000 had gathered to protest against South Africa's racist apartheid laws and demand voting rights for the country's blacks, Asians and mixed-race people the government term Coloureds. Although mostly African, they included representatives from all racial groups, including 50 sympathetic whites. Shortly before the raid, special badges were presented to guests designated as outstanding 'Fighters For Freedom'. The only non-South African to receive a badge was Father Trevor Huddleston, a British Anglican missionary who has consistently defied apartheid rules and spoken out from his pulpit against the Nationalist Party regime.

JUNE 15

Hundreds Die In Anti-Peron Uprising

The streets of Buenos Aires became a battlefield this month as elements of Argentina's military tried to oust President Juan Peron from power. His regime, one of the more notoriously-corrupt in a corruption-riddled South America, has encountered the twin problems of runaway inflation and the enmity of an all-powerful Catholic Church. Matters came to a head on June 15 when Peron ordered two leading churchmen into exile. The Catholic Church has increased its attacks on him and his government since last December, when the president forced through a divorce law initiated by his dead wife, the legendary Evita. Two days later, rival army chiefs signalled the start of an armed uprising which pitted rebel troops and anti-Peron civilians against forces loyal to the president. More than 200 were reported killed in the first few days of battles which would soon spread to other cities.

Monroe's Seven-Year Triumph

A GALA NIGHT IN NEW YORK
as the new Marilyn Monroe movie *The Seven Year Itch* opened with due fanfares, floodlights - and rave reviews for her performance as the sexy but naive object of a married man's frustrated attentions.

The film's show-stopping scene - Marilyn luxuriating in the refreshing updraft of a subway airvent - would become one of the most enduring images of the tragic star and provide world poster manufacturers with income for life.

Ironically, it had been the filming of that sequence in a New York street which had enraged Marilyn's ex-baseball star husband Joe DiMaggio and pushed their already-rocky marriage into separation and divorce in October last year, after nine months of complete incompatibility.

MOTOR RACING:
EUROPE BANS GRAND PRIX ROAD RACES AS DEATH TOLL RISES

In a season dominated by the horrific events in Le Mans (see June news), the deaths of spectators during Italy's Mille Miglia race and the fatal crash in training of former world champion Alberto Ascari in May, a number of countries - France, Switzerland, Spain and Mexico included - outlawed racing as too dangerous, and the American Automobile Association withdrew from FIA, the international governing body.

There's no doubt that the new breed of Formula One cars had become too fast for racing safely on public road circuits, and a number of existing Grand Prix tracks would need extensive and expensive modifications if spectators were to be protected.

Britain and Italy (home of the Ferrari and Maserati teams) had not banned racing, so the British Grand Prix took place, as scheduled, at the new Aintree circuit in Liverpool. The Mercedes team's confidence in their lead drivers, world champion Juan Fangio and fast-rising Brit Stirling Moss, was justified when - to the delight of the 150,000 partisan crowd - the race was won by the home boy, with Fangio second.

In Monza, where £500,000 ($1.5m) had been spent in track refurbishment, rough concrete damaged suspensions and wheels, forced the withdrawal of Ferrari's Lancia D-50s before the event and contributed to Moss's terminal breakdown during the race, which Fangio duly won.

At season's end Mercedes announced their two-year involvement in Grand Prix racing was over. Although their stated reason was a need to focus research on production cars, there's no doubt events at Le Mans forced their decision.

The US racing fraternity was stunned too by the death of Bill Vukovich during his attempt to become three-times winner of the Indy 500. He was killed instantly when his new Kurtis-Offy KK500C piled into wreckage of a crash between Al Keller and Johnny Boyd, somersaulted into a car park and burst into flames.

The re-started race was won by Bob Sweikert, ironically in a Kurtis KK500C. Sweikert himself would die in 1956 from injuries sustained in a race on a half-mile track at Salem, Indianapolis.

SOCCER:
EUROPEAN CUP A REAL TRIUMPH

A long time coming, the European Champions Club Cup finally came into being this year, with sixteen clubs - not all of them national champions - invited to compete for the first pan-European trophy.

Typically, no English teams took part as the insular Football League ruled that the tournament would confuse the domestic fixture list, although Hibernian did carry the Scottish flag as far as the semi-finals. Their inclusion in a champions' championship was strange, given that they'd only managed fifth place in the previous season's domestic league.

Led and inspired by Alfredo DiStefano, Spanish champions Real Madrid scored 20 goals *en route* to their Paris final against Reims, when they overcame an early two-goal deficit to emerge 4-3 winners.

It marked the arrival of a legendary team which would go on to win the trophy an unprecedented five times in succession.

Stirling Moss finishing Italy's Mille Miglia.

GOLF:
PALMER TURNS PRO

With pretty well every worthwhile amateur title already under his belt, 24 year old Ohio-born Arnold Palmer's 36th hole victory over Robert Sweeney in the 1954 American Amateur Final at Detroit Country Club was the one which persuaded him he was ready to tackle the professional golf circuit.

Initially barred from taking prize money under a PGA rule which stipulated a six-month unpaid apprenticeship, Palmer established his presence on the world stage in 1955 with his first major tournament win - the Canadian Open, held at Weston, Toronto.

JULY

Success, But No Agreement, At First World Summit

THE FIRST POST-WAR SUMMIT of world leaders from both sides of the East-West divide ended in Geneva today with all involved declaring the conference an outstanding success, even though they managed to disagree about everything except that their foreign ministers would get round the table again later this year to see if Germany's future can't be settled.

Attending the historic session were President Eisenhower, Britain's Sir Anthony Eden, French premier Edgar Faure and Soviet PM Nikolai Bulganin. The Western leaders found Bulganin's delegation less icy than those headed in the past by dead dictator Josef Stalin, but ran up against the usual brick wall of Soviet inflexibility on key subjects to prove a Cold War thaw is still some way off.

Typical of that was Bulganin's complete rejection of the British-sponsored plan for free all-German elections leading to a peace treaty and unification. The USSR said this was impossible without the abolition of NATO. Bulganin also suggested that he would have preferred to discuss the continued enmity of Communist China and the Nationalist Chinese regime on Formosa.

Ruth Ellis Goes To Gallows

The appeal against her death sentence having been rejected by the Home Secretary, convicted murderer Ruth Ellis was hanged at London's Holloway Prison for Women today as a large crowd of anti-capital punishment protestors waited outside the gates.

British opinion is divided on the subject, with the pro-hanging lobby itself split over the question of women being hanged.

In the event, Ruth Ellis would be the last British woman to suffer the extreme penalty. Outrage at her death would give abolitionists the ammunition they needed to work away and engineer the abolition of the death penalty in 1965.

Disney's Dream World Opens For Kids Of All Ages

The ultimate fantasy of film-maker Walt Disney was realized today with the opening of Disneyland, a 160-acre dreamland for anyone ready to suspend their sophistication for a day and submerge themselves in a never-never land peopled by all the master cartoonist's best-loved creations.

The world's biggest amusement park, Disneyland is an architectural triumph which recreates many of the more fantastic worlds of his films, including castles, mountains, Mississippi river boats, moon rockets and an idealized Main Street USA.

Situated in Anaheim, south of Los Angeles, Disneyland is expected to draw more than five million visitors a year.

Born this month:
9: Steve Coppell, England international soccer player, now manager
18: Terry Chambers, rock drummer (XTC)
20: Desmond Douglas, England international table tennis champion
28: Christopher Warren-Green, violinist, leader of Philharmonia Orchestra

DEPARTURES

Died this month:
23: Cordell Hull, US statesman. US Secretary of State when Japanese attacked Pearl Harbor in 1941, awarded Nobel Peace Prize in 1945.

JULY 17

French Troops Quell Moroccan Riots

With a state of martial law declared after Morrocan nationalists surrounded the President-General and threatened his life, French troops in armoured cars tonight moved into the Medina, ancient walled city heart of Casablanca and stronghold of the pro-independence movement.

After a three hour battle in the Medina's cramped and alley-strewn streets, French commanders claimed themselves back in control, but reported that they had discovered the body of a Spanish teenager, apparently stoned to death by locals.

They are also trying to trace three other Europeans believed murdered by nationalist sympathizers in the riots which preceded the French military action. The situation in Morocco has deteriorated so badly, the French government has to find some form of compromise to head off worse problems.

JULY 7

New Safety Calls As Jet Pilot Killed

The future of Britain's prestigious annual Farnborough Air Show - an international showcase for the world's civilian and military aircraft manufacturers - appeared to hang in the balance today following the crash of a new supersonic Hawker Hunter fighter and the death of its pilot.

There were increased calls for new safety measures to protect the thousands of spectators who flock to the Royal Aircraft Establishment's airfield, about 40 miles west of London, for close-up views of new planes and watch some of them in flight.

Critics invoked memories of the 1952 tragedy when 26 Farnborough visitors were killed by the wreckage of a De Havilland 110 jet fighter which exploded during an exhibition flight. Although no spectators were involved this time, it's suggested it was only a matter of luck. Next time, who knows?

JULY 2

Gulbenkian's Millions For Charity

Everyone knew that oil industry pioneer Calouste Gulbenkian was rich, but until family lawyers announced the terms of his will in the Portuguese capital, Lisbon, today no-one was sure exactly how rich he had been.

Two days after he died, they revealed that the Armenian-born Gulbenkian had left a tidy £300 million (that's $900m then, and about $4,500m in today's terms) to establish a foundation fund which will be devoted to art, education and charity.

The main beneficiaries of Gulbenkian's generosity will be the countless thousands of young Third World students who would be able to call on the foundation's funds to study in leading American, British and French universities.

Campbell Smashes World Water-Speed Record

THE WORLD WATER-SPEED RECORD was smashed today on Cumberland's Lake Ullswater when Donald Campbell powered his turbo-jet hydroplane *Bluebird* through two runs to clock up an average speed of 202.32 mph (325.53kph).

Campbell, the 34 year old son of former land and water speed record-holder the late Sir Malcolm Campbell, was typically modest about his achievement. Describing his adventure, which was witnessed by large crowds lining the lakeside, as 'primarily scientific', Campbell claimed: 'We are much more concerned with research and the general behaviour and design of craft...than we are with merely breaking the world's record'.

Queen's Portrait Breaks Royal Academy Records

ALWAYS A BIG CROWD-PULLER, The Royal Academy Summer Exhibition set new records this month as hundreds of thousands packed the venerable London art centre to catch a glimpse of the dramatic new portrait of Queen Elizabeth by Italian painter Pietro Annigoni.

More than 250,000 have already visited this year's month-long show which follows the tradition of hanging new works by acknowledged modern masters alongside those submitted for selection by wannabes and weekend amateurs.

The main attraction depicts the Queen in the dramatic cloak of The Order of The Garter against a romantic rural scene. The result of a number of sittings the Queen gave the Florence-based artist in 1954, it's been a huge hit with the public but dismissed as a display of emotionless technique by a number of critics.

London Audiences Don't Wait For Godot

Hailed as a 'Theatre of the Absurd' masterpiece when it opened in Paris two years ago, Irish-born Samuel Beckett's play Waiting For Godot was greeted with catcalls and the sound of seats flipping up when it opened at London's tiny Arts Theatre Club tonight.

Directed by 24 year-old newcomer Peter Hall, the French-based playwright's work - a series of surreal dialogues between two tramps (Godot himself never shows) got short shrift from first-night critics.

One said it tried 'to lift superficiality to significance through absurdity', while another pronounced: 'As far as I am concerned, the Paris intelligensia can have it back'!

German Genius Mann Dies In Exile

Thomas Mann, Germany's greatest 20th century novelist and man of letters, died today in Zurich, Switzerland, his home in exile since copies of his books were burned by order of the Nazis in the late 1930s. He was 79 years old.

His finest work was the novella *Death In Venice (Der Tod in Venedig)*. This - along with his 1925 mystical masterpiece *The Magic Mountain (Der Zauberberg)* - helped win him the 1929 Nobel Prize for Literature.

A ferocious anti-fascist, Mann used his 1947 novel *Dr Faustus* to mirror the rise and fall of the Hitler regime, while his *Confessions of Felix Krull* in 1953 dealt more directly with the subject by reflecting German family life through the 1918-1945 period.

British Boroughs Get Green Belt Order

British housing minister Duncan Sandys became the friend of conservationists today when he ordered 140 local authorities to limit the future spread of their towns and cities by setting up so-called Green Belts.

Using already-established legislation in place to ensure that London does not continue to swallow up vast tracts of farmland and open countryside, Mr. Sandys ordered the authorities to draw up and submit current boundary plans and introduce Green Belt legislation as soon as possible.

Existing boundaries are intended to form invisible barriers which authorities and developers cannot breach without a long series of planning applications and hearings which will eventually reach national government level.

Demonstrations in the streets of Delhi against the death of un-armed protesters in Goa

AUGUST 4

Bulganin's Niet To Ike's Inspection Suggestion

It's all very well for all sides to agree in principle that it would be a good thing if the superpowers scaled down their immense stockpiles of weapons, not only to make the world a theoretically safer place, but to reduce the vast amounts it costs to create those stockpiles.

The trouble is, no-one trusts anyone else to honour the agreements they agree should be signed so those funds can be used for hospitals, schools, housing, and other social infrastructures which would enrich people's lives.

President Eisenhower thought he had the answer: a mutual inspection procedure for military establishments. Russians could check American, British and French bases and installations as long as US, British and French inspectors were given the same access to Soviet facilities. Simple and sensible.

Too sensible and simple for members of the Supreme Soviet. They vetoed the idea outright, leaving Prime Minister Nikolai Bulganin with the job of rejecting Ike's proposal out of hand in Moscow today.

Gaza Conflict Reaches Stalemate

The stand-off between Israel and Egypt over the disputed Gaza Strip territory occupied by Egyptian forces for the past six years, simmered to boiling point this month. On August 24, the talks aimed to settle the dispute fell apart when Egyptian delegates walked out of a scheduled session.

In an increasingly tense atmosphere, Egyptian and Israeli fighters clashed over Gaza for the first time since 1948, when new national borders were agreed. That border has been the subject of sporadic armed confrontation since Israel mounted a retaliatory raid in February.

On August 31 Egypt reluctantly accepted a UN-policed ceasefire in the border region. It would be four days before the Israeli government agreed to take part. In truth, the real trouble was only just beginning.

Indian Protestors Shot By Police In Goa

ON WHAT WAS SUPPOSED to be a national holiday to celebrate the anniversary of independence from Britain, India was today mourning the death of 12 non-violent protestors demanding that Portugal hand back Goa, the west coast enclave it retains as a colony. They were shot by Goan police as they attempted to cross the border.

Among those wounded, either by police fire or at the hands of stave-bearing Goan citizens who attacked protestors, was V.D.Chitale, the incursion's communist leader. He had appealed for Indian Prime Minister Pandit Nehru to take a tougher line in talks with the Portuguese, and while Nehru also insisted that Goa was an integral part of India, he would not use Indian forces to seize the enclave.

Portuguese response to an official Indian protest was immediate and obdurate. It blamed 'grave acts of violation of sovereignty' for the shootings and said responsibility for casualties belonged entirely to those who had 'excited, consented to and favoured the invasion'.

Nehru had no real alternative. On August 20 he declared that India had broken off diplomatic relations with Portugal, making the quest for Goa's return to Indian rule official government policy.

Death Toll Mounts As Algerians Riot

More than 500 people were reported killed and another 226 injured in Algeria today as thousands of armed independence-seeking nationalists launched simultaneous attacks on French police and military targets.

The small coastal town of Philippeville was the setting for one typical, but especially-bloody confrontation between French militia and an invading crowd armed with automatic weapons, knives and axes.

Although the town's population was a mere 6,000, the French counter-attack left more than 100 rioters dead and 300 taken prisoner.

Staged to mark the second anniversary of France's deposing Sidi Mohammed Ben Youssef, former Sultan of Morocco, the riots were also planned to coincide with an uprising of Moroccan nationalists seeking more than the internal autonomy recently offered them by the French.

Jacques Soustelle, Governor-General, flew to the local nationalist stronghold of Constantine to oversee the enforcement of what he described as an 'uneasy truce'. That proved to be optimistic, and the Algerian death toll passed the 1,000 mark after only two more days of insurrection, at which point the French government opened full-scale peace talks.

ROSE MARIE GIVES YODELLIN' SLIM HIT OF DECADE

Although the 1950s have rightly gone down in history as the rock 'n' roll decade, it would be unfair not to pay tribute to a man who established a remarkable record this year - one which would stand unbroken for an amazing 36 years.

The man was Florida-born country and western yodeller Slim Whitman, and his achievement was to rack up no less than 11 consecutive weeks at No.1 in the British charts with his ballad *Rose Marie* and so beat the year-old record of 10 weeks set by English crooner David Whitfield's trans-Atlantic hit *Cara Mia*.

Even though Whitman's feat would be rivalled many times through the years - most closely by the nine weeks rung up in 1957 by Paul Anka's *Diana,* by Queen's *Bohemian Rhapsody* in 1975-76, Wings' *Mull Of Kintyre* in 1977-78, *You're The One That I Want* by John Travolta and Olivia Newton-John in 1978, and by Frankie Goes To *Hollywood's Two Tribes* in 1984 - it would not be until 1991 and Bryan Adams' humungous 16 weeks at the top with *(Everything I Do) I Do It For You,* that Slim's record would fall.

Whitman would go on to have further UK hits in 1955, with *Indian Love Call* and *China Doll,* and score a handful of others over the next three years. His old-fashioned style of country music was miraculously revived in 1974 when a TV-promoted *Best Of* compilation album became Britain's best-selling LP and the 50 year old scored a Top 20 single hit with *Happy Anniversary* to revitalize his concert and touring career.

Slim Whitman: No. 1 with Rose Marie

HALEY ROCKS, BUT ALMOST ALONE

The arrival in the US charts of Bill Haley & The Comets' *Rock Around The Clock* in May this year, and its long run as America's biggest-seller of 1955, had world-shattering implications for popular music. It would be wrong to describe it as the moment rock 'n' roll was born, however, and just as wrong to assume that it resulted in an immediate deluge of the same.

Truth is, while the Detroit-born, former western swing singer's hit did open the major record companies' eyes to the commercial potential of this new sound, they took their time developing and releasing it.

Meanwhile, as the kids knew only too well, small independent labels had been delivering the goods for some time. What the industry was calling rock 'n' roll had been around for a couple of years, if you knew where to tune your radio, and there were many as-yet-unknowns who'd notched up regional hits with their blend of blues, R&B and country.

In major chart success terms, Bill Haley had the field pretty much to himself until July, when boy-next-door Pat Boone scored with his sanitized version of Fats Domino's R&B classic *Ain't That A Shame*, and a young black guitarist called Chuck Berry had his first national hit with *Maybellene*.

WANT A HIT?
GET A (COONSKIN) HAT!

An immediate hit with American TV viewers when it began early in 1955, the Walt Disney-produced *Adventures of Davy Crockett* series not only gave Texas-born actor Fess Parker the biggest break of his career as the frontier hero 'born on a mountain-top in Tennessee' who'd 'killed him a bear when he was only three'. It also created an international craze for the distinctive coonskin hat worn by Parker/Crockett, and resulted in an almighty rush to record the show's signature song.

First off the blocks was Bill Hayes, whose version raced into the US charts at No.5 in March, and by April was lodged firmly in the top spot. Hot on his heels was Fess Parker himself (in at No.15) and the aptly-named and

big-voiced Tennessee Ernie Ford (a first-entry at No.20).

At one stage, in April, all three were Top 10 fixtures - a unique achievement for any song. But the saga hadn't ended.

Not released in Britain until 1956 when the TV show was eventually picked up, the UK battle with *The Ballad Of Davy Crockett* was won by Bill Hayes again, with Tennessee Ernie Ford (also scoring hugely with his former US No.1 *Sixteen Tons*) runner-up and Parker not in the frame. He wasn't alone, though. Among those who also released covers in Britain were Burl Ives, Steve Allen, Fred Waring's Pennsylvanians, Gary Miller, Ronnie Ronalde, Dick James, Max Bygraves and Billy Cotton!

UNCHAIN A MELODY SMASH

Destined to become a pop classic and become (often unwisely!) one of the most-recorded songs of all time, *Unchained Melody* first caused spines to tingle in April when an orchestral version by Capitol Records staff arranger Les Baxter shot into the US Top 10. The Texas-born musician couldn't have known what he'd started with the main title theme of the movie *Unchained*.

Within days his eventual No.2 had been joined in the charts by a vocal version by former Duke Ellington Orchestra singer Al Hibbler, and by June they were being pursued by Roy Hamilton, who'd had his first big hits in 1954 with Rodgers and Hammerstein's *You'll Never Walk Alone* and *Ebb Tide*.

British music lovers were just as quick to spot a winner, and while Les Baxter's original did chart through May-July, the real tussle for the top was between Al Hibbler and local boy Jimmy Young. Although Hibbler stole an early lead to reach No.2 in June, by July it was the future BBC star DJ who'd taken over, racking up an impressive 19 weeks in the UK Top 20.

SEPT

Heart Attack Rules Out Second Term For Ike?

ALTHOUGH THE HEART ATTACK suffered in his sleep last night by President Eisenhower is described by his doctors as 'moderate', American political commentators believe it inevitably means that Ike will not seek a second term of office in 1956.

The 60 year old President's coronary took everyone by surprise. A naturally ebullient and physically-active man (evidenced by his fondness for golf), those same commentators blame the rigours of office on his illness. The prediction game is destined to continue during the seven weeks Eisenhower spent recuperating, but will be entirely disproved when he not only ran for office in 1956, but returned to The White House with a hugely increased share of the popular vote.

For the time being, Ike lies in an oxygen tent at the Fitzsimmons Army Hospital, Denver, his condition described as 'satisfactory'. At his bedside is his wife Mamie, due to be joined tomorrow by Vice-President Richard Nixon.

Among the first of thousands of get-well messages which flooded into the hospital were those from former British Prime Minister, wartime friend and peacetime ally Sir Winston Churchill, and Field Marshal Bernard Montgomery, the argumentative thorn in Ike's side during the same period.

Burgess And Maclean Confirmed As Spies

Confirming what everyone had known since their disappearance in May 1951, but they had previously refused to admit, the British Foreign Office today announced that diplomats Guy Burgess and Donald Maclean were Soviet agents and had fled to Moscow when they realized they were under suspicion.

The FO's statement came in response to a newspaper article by Vladimir Petrov, the Soviet diplomat who defected to Australia in July 1954 and had spent the intervening year spilling the beans on Russia's intelligence operations in the West.

While the FO refused to confirm Petrov's claim that Burgess (44) and Maclean (42) had been recruited by Soviet intelligence while they were students at Cambridge University, it admitted that both of the Washington-based diplomats had been under investigation when they boarded the Southampton-St.Malo ferry to begin their flight to Moscow.

It only remains to be seen if they acted alone or, as the London-Washington rumour mill has it, there was a third man involved.

General Strike Hits Cyprus

Communications across the riot-torn British-ruled island of Cyprus were crippled today as a general strike began. The strike was called by supporters of EOKA, the outlawed organization seeking union with Greece.

Gangs of youths stoned Cypriot police and British forces who tried to break up anti-British demonstrations, and while troops were ordered to shoot to kill if necessary, no serious casualties were reported as hundreds of EOKA members were arrested.

Hughie Doubles Contestants' Money

British opponents of commercial television were quick to voice smug 'Told you so!' condemnations tonight as ITV screened the first *Double Your Money* (pictured), an American-created quiz show destined to become one of the UK's most popular programmes during the next 13 years.

Inspired by *The $64,000 Question* (although its biggest-possible prize was £1,000), the show was hosted by the fast-talking, brash and bouncy Hughie Green, a Canadian-born former child actor who'd served with the Royal Air Force during WWII.

As far as its critics were concerned, *Double Your Money* was ample proof that commercial TV would hasten the end of civilization as we knew it.

SEPTEMBER 22

Classic BBC Spoiler Mars ITV Launch

Everyone knew that the BBC - until today the only source of TV and radio in Britain - would do something to steal the thunder of the first two commercial TV stations as they came on-air tonight. But everyone assumed they'd do it via television.

The BBC's master-stroke was to use one of the brightest stars in their radio firmament to generate the next morning's headlines. They achieved it in aces by simply killing off one of the central characters in their most popular radio soap, The Archers, only minutes before the new TV rivals began their inaugural mix of variety shows, drama and boxing. First broadcast in 1951 (and still running five times a week to this day), The Archers boasted an audience of 10 million who hung on every twist and turn in the lives of the farming Archer family. Killing Grace, the young wife of Archer son and heir Phil, in a barn blaze was audacious timing the BBC claimed was 'pure coincidence'.

Whatever, it dented the impact of the London-based Associated Rediffusion and Associated Broadcasting Company's first nights. For the record, the first ad ever shown on British TV was for Gibbs' SR toothpaste.

SEPTEMBER 24

Peron Flees Argentina

President Juan Peron, for the past 10 years dictator of Argentina, was tonight granted asylum by the ruling junta in Paraguay after being ousted by a *coup* led by a group of army and navy commanders and greeted enthusiastically by cheering crowds.

Although small pockets of Peron supporters continue to fight on, their former leader's flight into exile aboard a Paraguayan gunboat leaves them rudderless.

Peron's power base finally began to crumble when he agreed to allow the Californian Standard Oil Company to develop Argentinian natural resources. But his attacks on the Catholic Church and open courtship of big business interests had eroded his popularity with the 'shirtless poor' who'd originally swept him to

Death Crash Martyrdom For James Dean

ACTOR AND FAST-RISING teen idol James Dean gained instant immortality today when he died at the wheel of his Porsche Spyder *en route* to a road race near Los Angeles, California. He was, and therefore destined to remain, only 24 years old.

Dean, who was born near Indianapolis but moved with his dental mechanic father to Santa Monica at the age of six, shot to stardom in 1955 with two hit films - *East Of Eden* and *Rebel Without A Cause*. Both featured him in the role of a tortured misunderstood teenager, and both rang loud bells with a generation of youngsters who could identify completely with him and the characters he portrayed.

Discovered in 1954 by director Elia Kazan while appearing in a New York stage play, Dean was soon being compared with Marlon Brando. He had only recently finished work on his third, as yet unreleased, movie *Giant* with Rock Hudson and Elizabeth Taylor, and was celebrating the signing of a six-year, nine movie deal.

The hysterical grief which greeted his death and marked his funeral was comparable only with the scenes which accompanied the passing of silent movie star Valentino. Fan clubs sprang up worldwide to ensure that Dean's brooding presence remained a potent and permanent symbol of the rejection and victimization visited on teenagers by an unfeeling adult world.

power.

Another victim of Peron's fall was his dead wife, the once-popular Evita. Statues of her were torn down and dragged through the streets of Buenos Aires as victory celebrations began. On September 24, General Eduardo Lonardi was sworn in as provisional president to set the seal on Peron's defeat.

OCTOBER 8

Hitler Did Die In Bunker, Says Pilot

Ten years after Allied forces finally over-ran Berlin to end WWII in Europe, there are still some who aren't convinced that the cremated bodies found by Russian troops in the bunker occupied by Adolf Hitler were those of the Nazi dictator and his mistress, Eva Braun.

Surviving supporters of the Third Reich refuse to believe the Führer would commit suicide and choose to cling to the theory that he escaped into an exile from which he will one day return. Others doubt this because most of the physical evidence has lain in Soviet hands since then, with only their word to go on.

All conjecture and controversy appeared to be closed today with the return to West Germany of Hans Bauer, Hitler's personal pilot. Released from captivity in Russia, he confirmed that the bodies were those of Hitler and Eva. They had been set alight on orders given by Hitler before the couple swallowed poison to end what he had predicted would be a 1,000-year Reich.

South Africa Stages UN Walk-Out

THE WHITE-POWER GOVERNMENT of South Africa took its first major step towards international isolation today when its UN delegate, W.C. du Plessis, staged a walk-out protest against a General Assembly debate critical of the regime's apartheid policies.

Weary of repeated South African breaches of the UN human rights charter and its refusal to accept or concede to past UN criticism which has labelled apartheid 'a seriously disturbing factor in international relations', the General Assembly voted to debate the issue in full open session.

This, according to an apparently-outraged du Plessis, was an intervention in his country's internal affairs. It was also therefore a breach of the UN's founding charter.

South Africa's absence did not halt the debate, nor curtail the long stream of member nation delegates only too happy to deliver a series of uninterrupted attacks on a regime which treats the majority of its citizens as non-people, unable to live and work where they want, or to change the system by voting in elections reserved for those with white skins.

No New Channel Record For American Woman

Florence Chadwick, the American long-distance swimming ace who broke a 24 year old women's record in 1950 when she swam the 22 miles of the English Channel between the French mainland at Cap Gris Nez and the Kent port of Dover in only 13 hours 23 minutes, had long cherished a dream to reduce the record even more.

Battling against increasingly choppy seas and mounting winds, she disappointingly recorded a time 30 minutes slower.

Cheered ashore by a large crowd of well-wishers, Chadwick at least completed her second run - more than can be said for fellow American Shirley France, her companion in 1950. Back then she was pulled from the sea eight miles from the English coast, hysterical and blue with cold.

NEWS IN BRIEF

17: In London, British European Airways ordered a fleet of *Vanguard* turbo-prop airliners, to be built by Vickers-Armstrong

26: In Hollywood, world premiére of *Rebel Without A Cause,* James Dean's second film, which co-starred Natalie Wood and Sai Mineo *(see picture)*

BBC Unveils Colour TV

The BBC went on the offensive against its new commercial television rivals today at its Alexandra Palace studios in north London, when it staged an impressive demonstration of the colour quality it says it will introduce to all regions in the next few years.

Experts were impressed by the accuracy and brilliance of the images shown, although they did express doubts about the cost to customers, all of whom will have to buy new sets to receive the broadcasts. The day before, the BBC announced it had expanded its production facilities hugely by purchasing the Ealing Film Studios in West London, home of the legendary Ealing comedies which helped establish the international careers of Alec Guinness and Peter Sellers, among others.

OCTOBER 30

Princess Margaret: I Will Not Marry Peter Townsend

A CLASSIC BATTLE between love and duty ended today with a victory for duty when Princess Margaret put an end to months of speculation by announcing that she would not, after all, be marrying her lover, Group Captain Peter Townsend (pictured), a divorced RAF fighter pilot who'd been an aide to her late father, King George VI.

The insurmountable barrier confronting their union was Townsend's prior marriage. The Church of England does not recognize divorce and Margaret, third in the line of succession to the British throne and therefore a potential nominal head of the Church, could not have a divorced consort.

The 25 year old Princess was free to marry without the Queen's consent, but to do so would strip her of Civil List payments made to members of the Royal Family, and her place in succession.

In the face of opposition from the government, The Duke of Edinburgh and her mother, Princess Margaret sought guidance from the Archbishop of Canterbury on October 27 and finally decided not to buck the system.

Her statement reflected his advice by saying she was '...mindful of the Church's teaching that Christian marriage is indissoluble'. Conscious of her duty to the Commonwealth, Princess Margaret concluded: 'I have resolved to put these considerations above all others.'

Appointed to King George's staff in 1944, the dashing Group Captain and Princess Margaret had become immediate good friends, but it was not until 1953 that their romance became an open secret. They were separated by his posting to Brussels as an Air Attaché - a move ordered by Margaret's alarmed family.

It was a tragic end to what had been a real fairy-tale romance.

OCTOBER 19

Grim Cost Of Mau Mau Revealed

When a struggle between terrorists and the forces of law and order drags on for an extended period - as it has done now in Kenya for close on three years as the nationalist Mau Mau organization waged its bloody war against white settlers, African enemies and rivals, and the British army and air force - it's all to easy to lose sight of the real cost to human life.

Figures released in Nairobi today brought the truth home with a terrible jolt. The death count over those three years is an appalling 13,000.

Just as chilling is the fact that more than 70,000 Mau Mau and suspected supporters of the mostly Kikuyu tribe movement, have been rounded up and imprisoned in that time. These include many Mau Mau leaders, most notably Jomo 'Burning Spear' Kenyatta, who now live in prison compounds in remote mountain areas.

OCTOBER 28

Geneva Deadlock As Big Four Meet

The slight thaw in East-West relations which commentators believed marked the August summit of US, Soviet, British and French leaders, returned to a big freeze in Geneva today when foreign ministers of the 'Big Four' nations quickly hit a deadlock in discussions intended to find accord on European security.

Russia's Foreign Minister, Vyacheslav Molotov, set the tone - and the talks into immediate stalemate - when he firmly ruled out the West's proposals for German reunification and countered with a demand for the dissolution of both NATO and the Warsaw Pact signed by Eastern bloc countries in May.

American Secretary of State John Foster Dulles pleaded in vain for Molotov to see the importance of the US pledge to underwrite the European non-aggression treaties which the Soviets refused to sign.

Molotov also refused to accept the argument of British foreign minister Harold Macmillan that the West could not accept that giving security to Russia must lead to giving up its own defenses by dissolving NATO.

GREG NORMAN

One of the most popular and successful golfers of the past 20 or so years, the tall Queensland-born Australian - whose sun-bleached hair won him the nickname 'The White Shark' - earned his popularity via an obvious and infectious enthusiasm for the game he didn't take up until the age of 17, and his ability to recover from the many disasters his wilful enthusiasm have created along the way.

The son of a mining manager, Norman was a natural athlete and played the bruising Rugby League and Australian Rules Football as a teenager. His abiding love of the physical means he spends his spare time hunting (occasionally crocodiles), surfing, scuba diving and watching his long-time mate Nigel Mansell burn up race tracks.

Emerging as 1976 victor of the West Lakes Classic in Adelaide after only 16 months as a trainee pro, Norman was 'adopted' by 50s golf star Peter Thomson, selected to represent Australia in the 1977 World Cup in California, and within a year had won his first European event.

By 1980 Norman had conquered the Japanese circuit and was concentrating on gaining his PGA Tour card to focus on the USA. Within four years Norman was winning American tournaments regularly and collecting winnings of $310,230. By 1986 he'd won his first major, the British Open at Turnberry, and increased his season's earnings to $653,296.

Turnberry apart, Norman always seemed to blow up in major tournaments, even if he was runner-up in the 1986 and 1987 US Masters. His fan club remained loyal despite a 27-month American tour drought which ended with a Canadian Open victory in 1992.

Albert Einstein

Since then Norman has regained his Sony world No.1 ranking from Nick Faldo by winning the Doral Open, the British Open and the Johnny Walker Classic and adding $1,393,653 to his bank account in 1993 alone.

APRIL 18
ALBERT EINSTEIN

For a scientist to become a household name, it's usual for him/her to have invented something everyday-useful (non-stick fry-pans, superglue, instant potato mash), or become a media star capable of explaining weird stuff (quantum physics, cosmic phenomena) in language which even Beavis and Butthead can understand.

Which makes it remarkable that German-born physicist Albert Einstein, who died today in Princeton, New Jersey aged 76, is probably the most famous scientist of the 20th Century. He invented nothing and his research led to the kind of books which need a PhD to get you past the contents page.

Born in Ulm and educated in Germany and Switzerland, he took a job in the Swiss patent office to enable him to carry out the research which led to the publication, in 1905, of three major papers - one of them The Theory of Special Relativity - which would give the lead for the development of modern physics.

Awarded professorships in Zurich and Berlin, he won a Nobel Prize in 1921 for his work on the photo-electric effect. In 1930 he began lecturing in California, and remained in the US after Hitler's rise to power in 1933. As a Jew, Einstein knew he had no future in Germany, and took up a post at the Institute of Advanced Study in Princeton, where he remained until his death.

Although his research into uranium fission was invaluable to the team which created the atomic bomb, Einstein worked tirelessly to warn world leaders of the dangers implicit in nuclear arms and became a vocal supporter of the Campaign for Nuclear Disarmament.

And, along the way, he became a household name and his Theory of Relativity became one of those things everyone knew about, even if they didn't know what it actually was!

MARCH 28
REBA MCENTIRE

One of the most successful female country music performers of the past 20 years, Reba McEntire was born today in Chockie, Oklahoma, daughter of a world champion rodeo steer-roper.

A promising rodeo performer in her teens, she also proved a popular singer with local bands. The two came together in 1974 when she was invited to sing the national anthem to start the National Rodeo Finals and country star Red Steagall persuaded her to give up her plans of a teaching career in elementary schools and cut a demo tape in Nashville instead.

Signed to a major deal, Reba began making an unbroken string of hit singles and albums which, apart from giving her trophy rooms full of gold and platinum disks, won her the Country Music Association's Female Vocalist of the Year in 1984, '85 and '86, a 1987 Grammy Award (for her song *Whoever's In New England*) and innumerable fan poll awards.

Tragedy struck in 1991 when eight members of her band were killed in a plane crash in California. Like any good rodeo rider would, Reba overcame that awful blow by returning to the world stage as soon as she could, gaining even more fans in the process.

Cyprus State Of Emergency As Governor Escapes Death

AS BRITISH TROOPS and local police fought an increasingly bitter battle with Greek Cypriots of the nationalist EOKA movement, the island's Governor, Sir John Harding today declared a state of emergency - and missed death when he failed to attend a ball at which four guests were injured by a bomb blast.

Sir John's announcement, which gives him the authority to introduce and enforce any regulation he believes necessary to ensure public order, and the government a series of draconian powers to crack down on EOKA, comes only two days after another two British soldiers died in terrorist attacks to raise the death toll in the past month to five.

Among the powers adopted by Sir John are the ability to impose censorship and curfews, detain or deport suspected terrorists and to confiscate property. The death penalty can be awarded anyone found guilty of discharging firearms at another, throwing or laying bombs, and possessing guns, ammunition or explosives.

The state of emergency was immediately attacked by Archbishop Makarios III, the Greek Orthodox primate who has emerged as spiritual and political leader of the movement calling for Cypriot union with Greece. Predicting it would make the crisis more acute, he accused Sir John of trying to bend the resistance of the Cypriot people.

Sir John's escape came this evening. Engrossed in the crisis, he decided not to attend the Caledonian Society Ball at Nicosia's Ledra Palace Hotel. Troops searching the post-explosion debris found an unexploded grenade under the table reserved for the Governor's party.

New German Army Born In Garage

The ceremony was brief and casual, and the setting was something else. West Germany's new army was founded today in the garage of the Ministry of Defense in Bonn, where the first 101 soldiers of the infant force were commissioned by Defense Minister Theodor Blank.

Reinforcing the surprisingly *ad hoc* nature of the event, only 12 of those invested actually wore uniforms. Ending 10 years of demilitarization, the West German army is to be led by Lieutenant-General Heusinger and General Speidel. Russian suspicions (and French concerns) with German rearmament are only heightened by the fact that Heusinger was Adolf Hitler's wartime Operations Chief, while Speidel - now Bonn's representative at NATO - was one of Field Marshal Rommel's henchmen.

USSR Explodes Biggest H-Bomb

Soviet leader Nikita Khrushchev today confirmed what Western scientists and military chiefs already knew from seismograph readings - the USSR recently exploded what he described as its 'most powerful' hydrogen bomb yet.

The device, claimed by Khrushchev to be the equivalent of a megaton (one million tons) of TNT, was part of tests being carried out 'in the interests of national security'.

Khrushchev used the announcement - and the implied threat of the USSR's increased nuclear capabilities - to restate his proposals for the prohibition of nuclear weapons and the 'establishment of effective international control'.

NOVEMBER 12

British Two-Wheelers Take On The Imports

The main hall of London's Earls Court exhibition centre became a unique battleground today as British motorcycle manufacturers replied to the barrage of successful imported mopeds and scooters with a collection of UK-made rivals.

Most of the popular imports are Italian. While their biggest sales go to mopeds, the sleek scooters made by Lambretta and Vespa have been capturing most of a fast-growing new market.

The British answer to the seven new foreign mopeds unveiled at this year's Cycle Show was the launch of nine domestic machines. On the scooter front, the Brit-built Dayton Albatross - capable of cruising at 50 mph (80kph) with a thrifty fuel consumption of 84 miles (129km) to the gallon - was declared a very handsome contender.

53

MP Accuses Kim Philby Of Being 'Third Man'

DRAMATIC MOMENTS in the House of Commons today as the Labour MP Colonel Marcus Lipton withdrew allegations he'd made only days earlier that Harold 'Kim' Philby - a former First Secretary at the British Embassy in Washington - was the 'third man' rumoured to have been involved in the disappearance of Soviet spies Guy Burgess and Donald Maclean.

Speaking to pressmen at his Kensington apartment, Philby admitted to having had an 'imprudent friendship' with Burgess since they'd met at Cambridge University in the 1930s. He'd also met Maclean during that time, but claimed he was 'only a shadow in my memory'. A strange claim, given that Burgess and Maclean had been such bosom buddies and Philby had succeeded Maclean to the Washington Post.

Philby and Burgess had lived together in Washington before Burgess returned to London in 1951 but, Philby claimed: 'The last time I spoke to a Communist, knowing he was one, was in 1934'. One assumes he didn't include in that statement the hundreds of Soviet officials he must have dealt with as a diplomat. He also denied ever having been a Communist, 'although I knew people who were Communists at Cambridge and for a year afterwards', For the record: Marcus Lipton was finally proved right in 1963 when Kim Philby defected to Moscow and admitted he'd been a Soviet agent since 1933. He died in 1988.

US Play Both Ends In Mid-East Game

American diplomats had a busy month of it as far as the Middle East was concerned, and tried to walk the thin line of neutrality between the implacably opposed governments of Israel and Egypt by giving both governments most of what they wanted.

The first moves came on November 2, when David Ben-Gurion - one of Israel's founding fathers and a leading fighter for nationhood in the 1940s - became the new prime minister. His arrival led the way to a November 7 announcement in Washington that the US would sell arms to Israel, a move it had previously refused to make.

With tension between Israel and Egypt in the disputed Gaza Strip region at constant breaking point as troops from both sides broke cease-fire agreements, the Eisenhower administration had to act positively and quickly to ensure continued dialogue with the Egyptian regime of Colonel Nasser.

This was achieved on November 20 when talks began in Washington to discuss US aid towards financing the vast dam Nasser plans to build on the River Nile at Aswan. Crucial to his modernization plans, a substantial American donation would help make the dam a reality - and help soften the blow of those arms sales to Israel.

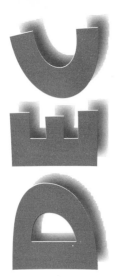

Attlee Moves To Lords, Gaitskell To Lead Labour

WORN OUT BY YEARS of internal party strife and the sheer hard work of presiding over six years of massive social reform following his 1945 election victory, Labour Party leader Clement Attlee resigned today. Within hours he accepted a knighthood from the Queen and moved to the House of Lords.

The 72 year old's departure announcement was typical of a man best described as shy and unassuming. At a meeting of Labour members of parliament, he said: 'Before you turn to important business, I have a personal statement. I want to end uncertainty over future leadership. I am resigning.'

Behind Attlee's self-effacing façade was an accomplished wheeler-dealer. He times his resignation to give Shadow Chancellor Hugh Gaitskell - his personal choice as successor over his own deputy, Herbert Morrison - the best possible chance of winning the job.

So it would prove. On December 14, the 49 year old Gaitskell became the new Labour Party leader, polling 157 of votes cast by fellow MPs and socialist peers to the 70 of Aneurin Bevan and Herbert Morrison's 30 votes.

A tearful Morrison, chief architect of Labour's 1945 landslide victory, immediately announced his resignation as deputy leader. Aneurin Bevan pledged loyalty to the new right-wing leader, but it was an open secret that he and his hard-core socialist followers intended to give Gaitskell the toughest time imaginable.

Earl Attlee (left) and Hugh Gaitskell (right)

Good Read In '55

A year-end review of the book world throws up a number of notables. If headlines mean anything, 1955 was Vladimir Nabokov's year. His novel Lolita scandalized decent folk everywhere as it recounted a middle-aged academic's fixation with and seduction of his 13 year old stepdaughter. Defended by highbrows for its graceful literary style, it was snapped up by countless lowbrows searching it fruitlessly for obscenities or descriptions of the sexual act. Sex played a large part in the life and exploits of Agent 007, James Bond. Avid readers of Ian Fleming's creation, who first emerged in 1953 with Casino Royale, were not disappointed with this year's offering, Moonraker, which pitted Bond against baddie Hugo Drax, lots of other heavies, and a number of beautiful women only too happy to let Bond have his way with them.

Inquiry Launched Into London Train Fire

An official government inquiry was ordered by the government in London today while fire and rescue workers searched the wreckage of a commuter train in south-west London.

Twelve people died and 40 more were injured as fire swept through the train as it passed through the suburb of Barnes. Local rail staff and fire experts were horrified by the carnage which greeted inspection teams who rushed to the site.

UN Shuts Door On Japan

Although it accepted 16 new members during a special session held in New York today, the United Nations turned down the applications of Japan and Mongolia.

Japan's failure to gain membership of the world forum was due entirely to a continued USSR veto based on unresolved territorial disagreements with the Japanese government and pique at the United States' refusal to allow Mao Tse-Tung's mainland China to join alongside the Formosan-based Nationalist regime of Chiang Kai-Shek.

Mongolia's application was also subject to Western veto. Although notionally an independent country, the remote Asian nation is occupied and run by the Communist Chinese, with the USSR also taking a slice of the action.

DECEMBER 10

No Peace Prize In Nobel Awards

It's not unique, but it is extremely rare for the Nobel Prize committee not to award the coveted Peace Prize to some international worthy, especially as it's an award which can be presented for a lifetime of diplomatic achievements. In 1954 the prize was given to the Office of the UN's High Commissioner for Refugees, something many believed was proof of the committee's desperation to name a recipient at all costs.

This year they admitted defeat and made no award, although some thought former French Prime Minister Pierre Mendes-France might have won it for bringing his country's bloody connections with Vietnam to an end and brokering the north-south split to establish some sort of stability between rival regimes.

DECEMBER 4

$14 Fine Leads To Black Bus Boycott In Alabama

THE $14 FINE IMPOSED on 42 year old black seamstress Rosa Parks in a Montgomery, Alabama court today lit the fuse for the first explosive confrontation between the South's established way of life and the aspirations of millions of people who are no longer prepared to accept being treated as second class citizens, or worse, because of their skin colour.

Mrs Parks' fine, for ignoring a bus driver's order to move to the back of the vehicle as required by Alabama's existing race laws, signalled the start of a complete and well-orchestrated boycott of Montgomery's City Lines Buses by thousands of blacks.

A spokesman for the boycotters said their protest would continue until people who rode the buses were no longer 'intimidated, embarrassed and coerced'. They were ready to meet local white civic leaders and the bus company to develop 'a more satisfactory and equitable transportation system'.

Although Mrs Parks' lawyers said they intended to appeal against her fine, they would not be drawn on whether they intended to attack the constitutional legality of segregation itself. The Supreme Court, which has already outlawed segregation in schools, is currently considering a similar South Carolina bus segregation case.

DECEMBER 29

Bulganin Claims ICBM

Soviet Premier Nikolai Bulganin threw down a fresh gauntlet in the Cold War today when he claimed the USSR had entered the inter-continental ballistic missile (ICBM) stakes.

If he's right, Russian military now has the capability, with its newest rocket, to deliver an H-bomb over 4,000 miles. Given the size of the Soviet Union and its communist satellites, there is nowhere on earth out of range of the most destructive weapon yet devised.

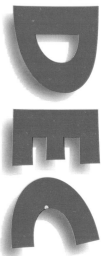

Cyprus Brits Form Home Guard

DECEMBER 22

Amid mounting bomb attacks and the random shooting of soldiers, members of the British business community in Cyprus today announced the formation of a Home Guard they hope will protect their families and homes from EOKA terrorists.

They have divided the capital Nicosia into command areas and have begun armed vigilante night patrols. The move comes in the wake of the recent shooting of two off-duty soldiers while doing their Christmas shopping, an EOKA retaliation for the arrest of 150 suspects in an island-wide clampdown on the Communist Party.

Bomb attacks on bars frequented by British troops have also increased, the worst resulting in 15 seriously injured soldiers. Local servicemen are now forbidden to use any bars, hotels or restaurants whose windows are not fitted with wire mesh.

YOUR 1955 HOROSCOPE

Unlike most Western horoscope systems which group astrological signs into month-long periods based on the influence of 12 constellations, the Chinese believe that those born in the same year of their calendar share common qualities, traits and weaknesses with one of 12 animals - Rat, Ox, Tiger, Rabbit, Dragon, Snake, Horse, Sheep, Monkey, Rooster, Dog or Pig.

They also allocate the general attributes of five natural elements - Earth, Fire, Metal, Water, Wood - and an overall positive or negative aspect to each sign to summarize its qualities.

If you were born between February 3, 1954 and February 16, 1955, you are a Horse. As this book is devoted to the events of 1955, let's take a look at the sign which governs those born between January 24 that year and February 11, 1956 - The Year of The Sheep.

THE SHEEP

JANUARY 24, 1955–
FEBRUARY 11, 1956
ELEMENT: WOOD   ASPECT: -

Sheep are socially, domestically and politically correct people, happy with the status quo, respect order and generally obey the rules and regulations society lays down.

The Year of the Sheep is characterized as a time of relative peace and tranquility because Sheep need harmony and usually go with the flow to maintain that harmony, contenting themselves with the consensus and playing the game.

Sheep have strong inherent herding instincts and function best as a part of a team, and members of that group lack individuality. Politically speaking, the Sheep is the sign of the moderate and the democrat, and it's precisely by keeping their heads and opinions down that Sheep manage to withstand and survive the many ups and downs of life.

Fortune favours the Sheep, possibly because they are so mild and unassuming they wouldn't be capable of using their own efforts and endeavours to make their own fortune. Consequently, luck helps make for an easy life where Sheep are concerned. If they are in public life, Sheep would be wise to have a reliable agent or manager to protect and promote them.

Sheep are tidy and appreciate ordered life and work environments. Males are particularly courteous and chivalrous, adhering to old-fashioned gentlemanly codes. However, while being passive and unoriginal creatures, they do like to show off - under a spotlight they can't resist turning into performers and showmen.

The sign of the Sheep is the most feminine and passive of all, and many female Sheep master and shine in arts and crafts. They have a keen eye for beauty and simply adore exquisite things. Psychologically, they need to be surrounded by beauty, for without pleasant and conducive surroundings they easily become depressed and dispirited.

It is essential for a Sheep - male and female - that they create a warm, harmonious and united domestic environment for themselves.

FAMOUS SHEEP

Muhammad Ali
World heavyweight boxing champion

Boris Becker
German tennis player

Ian Botham
cricket player

Terence Conran
British design guru, restauranteur

Catherine Deneuve
French film actress

John Denver
US singer, actor

Mikhail Gorbachev
Russian leader

Mick Jagger
Singer, songwriter, actor

Billie-Jean King
US tennis player, coach